BULLIES IN THE BOARDROOM

REBA JOHNSON

ISBN: 978-0-9998761-2-1

CONTENTS

A memoir of courage, faith, and attention to detail

1

I CHANGED THE NARRARATIVE

I was working as a student office assistant. I must have done a good job because right as I was leaving high school, Principal Dan told me that when I get my college degree to come back and as long as he was there, I would always have a job. So, in preparation, I took business management classes in college. But it's crazy how we never know for real what we're going to encounter in life. Sure enough…

I took a detour.

In junior college I fell in love with a basketball player named, Mark. I had spent too much time hanging out in the activity center waiting on him and playing ping pong. So, after two years, I had not earned my associates degree. But because Mark left that college, I left too. He transferred to Peoria, Il to play for the Bradley Braves basketball team. I transferred alright… with Walmart taking a fulltime position in Lincoln, Illinois. This was only about thirty minutes from where Mark was.

I could not find an affordable place to rent there in Lincoln especially with the few dollars I had. So, I watched TV, brushed my teeth, and washed up inside Walmart. But I ate snacks, changed clothes, and *slept* in my car. Some nights it was pretty hot in there. I made sure the windows were cracked for some ventilation. I had heard that sometimes God sends complete strangers to our rescue!

One day, as I was checking customers out on the register, a nice lady and her husband came through my checkout line. We chitchatted as I rang them up and bagged their merchandise. In the course of our conversation, we found out a couple facts about each other. I found out that he was a pastor, and that she was not only a first lady, but was pregnant! They found out that I was from Missouri, had just transferred there, and that I was a new homeless person in town, and pregnant, too.

The very next day, they came back to the store and came through my line again. I just figured that they forgot a few things like I do sometimes. But that was not the case. They had me rang up something to have an excuse to speak to me. But their real motive for coming straight back to my line was to offer me a place to *"lay my head."* The wife told me, *"No pregnant woman should be homeless, and you can stay with us as long as you need to."* I didn't know anything about the word, homeless. I just called it, sleeping in my car. But I moved in with them and stayed for a bit. They were very kind to me, and I paid them what I could.

I finally had saved enough money to move out and get my own apartment. But when I got ready to go, they did something that I was not expecting them to do. They returned all the money I had given them for letting me stay there! Talk about favor in the fire? That was such a blessing for me! My eyes lit up when they handed it to me!

As time went on, I moved back home to Missouri. Mark finally left college too and enlisted in the United States Marine Corp! We got married and he ended up stationed at Camp Lejeune. We lived there for a while. I got a part time job at Sears and Roebuck! That's where I learned and mastered my customer service skills. Eventually the kids and I went to live with his parents in Memphis. That was a blessing and quite an experience!

Because I knew that the world had more to offer than a retail or desk job, I decided that I would do something different. I applied for a job driving trucks for Coca Cola! Hot dog! Wouldn't you know it? The company told me that they *had* to start hiring women. So… they hired me and one other lady that day! I got my CDLs and was ready for the road! I became known in town as, The Coke Lady." At that moment, I felt fearless!

While driving trucks for them, I had several strange encounters! Every day I would sit up tall, straight, and proud as I wore my company-issued uniform! One day I was making a delivery at one of my favorite spots. I enjoyed stopping there because the owner was always jolly, had words of wisdom, helped me work that drop, and made me welcome to whatever snacks I wanted in his store. One day he even ran some young fellas off who were rocking my truck really hard trying to get it open. He ran them off with only one gun shot in the air! He didn't have to do all that. But it worked!

Another encounter happened at a different store. Mr. Glen was another very favorite customer and an awesome guy. Each day I would honk my horn a few times to let him know I was passing his store.

I had to go down to the end of the street to turn that big truck around so that the side door was facing his store. That just made things easier. Then once I made it back to the store, and walk in, he would always ask me, "You want the usual today, little lady?" I'd reply, "I sure do!" Then we would laugh, and we would say in unison, “Mustard and mayonnaise only, please.”

That particular day I sat at the end of the street for just a few minutes longer than usual reviewing my delivery log sheet. Finally, I headed back to Mr. Glen’s store to get my fried burnt bologna sandwich and sweet red Kool aid!

By the time I got back, police cars were swarming in! I got out of my truck trying to find out what was going on. The woman that Mr. Glen was dating was standing on the sidewalk hysterically speaking to two officers. She frantically beckoned for me to come to her.

With blood dripping from her hands, she was screaming of what had happened. Someone had shot Mr. Glen in the head and laid his head at the drain in the back room of his store, and she had found him. She was totally distraught and could hardly say what happened!

Another day as I was out making deliveries again, I started getting sick to my stomach. I thought it was because I hadn’t eaten breakfast. I hadn't been too long taken a physical for the year and assumed health wise, I was fine. I arrived at one of the grocery stores that I regularly served. It was on Chelsea Ave.

I drove up and parked my truck. When I went inside to check out the merchandising drop spot, the owner told me that I needed to call into my company ASAP. When I did, the voice on the other end of the phone told me not to make the drop and to come into the company office immediately.

On my way into the office, I couldn't help but wonder what in the world they needed to talk to me about. I knew many evenings I had come back into thc plant late from making deliveries and had driven upon just about all the sidewalks of every street in town. But I didn't think that was enough for them to let me go. So, what in the world could they want? I was feeling really hot around my coca cola collar.

When I walked in the boardroom, the fellas had a very strange look on their faces. They asked me to take a seat that they had something to discuss with me. They informed me that the company had gotten results back from my physical and that because I was pregnant, they could no longer allow me to drive for them. “PREGNANT!” I could not believe my ears!

But at that moment, I did something I hadn’t planned on doing before I left my house that morning. I maximized my seat at the conference table by changing the narrative! In addition to advocating for myself, I killed those fellas with kindness! They thought they were holding a Fire-a-Female-on-Friday kind of meeting. But they did not have a maternity leave clause written in the leave policy portion of the employee manual. They had not planned that far.

Funny thing about my time in college at Three Rivers. I might have spent too much time in the activity center to have enough credits to graduate. But I went to all my Business Management classes! I learned a few things there. First, not everyone gets invited to sit at the conference table. But, if you are blessed enough to get that chance, make sure you walk in on time, dressed appropriately, know the agenda, say what's most important, and own that room!

Well, I had four out of five of them. I was not ready to hear the agenda. "Mrs. Johnson, we're going to have to let you go." I listened to everything they had to justify the dismissal. I knew that if I was going to have any chance of keeping that job, I better talk up and talk up fast! So, I started out telling the powers that be what was in it for them, the company, and the stakeholders. Then, I made sure that I maintained a good attitude for the best possible outcome! That's how I begin to change the narrative.

I started with, "I greatly appreciate you all for giving me a chance to work here. Not all companies are being intentional and making sure they are hiring women and giving them a chance. I really like my job. So far, this has been an awesome company to work for and I'm proud to represent you guys."

After I used a few other fearless words, instead of just firing me, they decided to draw up leave of absence paperwork, effective immediately! They paid me for the rest of that day, my whole pregnancy, and even a long time after my delivery date. What a mighty God we serve! It didn't make up for the pallet of cokes that my supervisor dropped on my foot one day. I still have problems with it sometimes. I will always believe that the way it happened, he did it deliberately. I couldn't prove it, though. Nevertheless, my experience paved the way for other women who would come to work for the company.

2

I WAS PROACTIVE

Because I had no support there in Memphis at the time, I decided to go back to my hometown. Some would call that peddling backwards. I called it being courageous, leveraging myself, and being proactive for maximizing my seat at the next conference table. My mother came to my rescue! She helped me finish loading up my U-Haul and we hit the road! Since I had gotten the call from the company while I was making deliveries on Chelsea Avenue, I thought, "Well…if I have a baby girl, why not just name her, Chelsea?" So that's just what I did. I named her…Chelsey but with an *SEY*.

After Chelsey was old enough, I took a job with the Housing Authority. They erected me a new office right in the middle of the bottom floor. They even gave me a fancy name plate for my new desk! My supervisor made my job duties up as we went along. But a couple of things I was assigned to do was to attend building meetings and be on the Board of Directors for a new childcare facility being created. There was a lady named Maria. She was on the board of directors with me and was one of the nicest ladies I had met in a long time.

One day we visited a very well ran childcare program out of town. On the ride back, we talked about several things including my work there in housing. I didn't realize my potential.

But Ms. Maria did. Suddenly she interrupted me and said, "You seem like a really sharp girl. You should be doing something much more different than what you are doing. Would you like to connect with an organization that gives scholarships so that you can go back and finish your college degree? I put all my eggs in Ms. Maria's basket that day. She gave me a letter of recommendation and sooner than later, I applied for the Claudia Company Scholarship!

But wait a minute. Let me rewind and show you how God will give you courage and even help you to be fierce when you need to be!

I was working at the Housing Authority. My supervisor was a really tall red headed man! He had to be every bit of seven feet tall. He made a position for me telling me that off the record "there was a disproportional number of black employees." They created the job title of Family Services Coordinator. But for the most part, he made up my job duties as we went along. That should have been my first red flag.

Eventually, he began to have me do less and less of the job duties he had initially created and more and more of assignments that included me shadowing him. That should have been my second red flag. I should have known then he had an agenda. But nope. I was just excited that I was getting a chance to see more of what went on behind the scenes. Who knows? Maybe he was grooming me for a higher paying position.

Daily, we would go and check on the elderly in the high rise building who had not been seen for a few days. He also had me to accompany him a few times as we shopped for items for the offices. Again, he was my superior and I was a new employee. Nothing appeared too out of the ordinary. So, I would go as requested. His cordiality soon turned forceful and even harsh!

One particular day we went to Walmart. While there, we walked by a huge bin of comforters. We got only a few feet away and he stopped, walked back, and summoned me to step back as well. When I did, he pointed to one of the comforters and asked, "Which one of these would you like to have? At first, I said, "All of them! They are all really nice!" Then he said, "No seriously. I'll buy you one."

Now, *THAT* was weird and made me feel very uncomfortable! I told him, "Well neither one." He replied, "Oh come on. I will buy you any one you want as long as you let me come over and we romp in the sheets together." I told him that I was not interested. We walked away together. But I got lost in the store on purpose and just didn't go back to work with him that day.

But the next day, as always, I came to work dressed appropriately and professionally. He complimented me but never asked me what happened to me in Walmart? He just continued to make unwanted sexual advances. In spite of me telling him to stop and to keep things professional, he continued to say and do things that were not a part of the job. I kept deflecting him.

One day he came and asked me to go with him up to an elderly resident's apartment to check on them and to check on a couple other things. I didn't think anything of it as "checking" on things had begun to be part of my routine assignment. Once we got off the elevator, he had me follow him up steps. We continued until we made it to the top of the entire building. He opened a door that led to the rooftop.

First, he stepped out on to the roof top a little

way from the trap door. He spat off the side of the building not knowing or caring if his spit would land on someone walking by. I just stood right at the opening of the door. Instead of being on top of Old Smokey, I stood on the top of old Twin Towers. He stepped toward me, grabbed my arm, pulled me close to him and said, "It's time for us to handle a little personal business now." He was aggressive, too! I was so scared!

I jerked away and started back down through the trap door! I ran down the stairs tripping and bruising my legs and knees! Once I reached the director's office, I burst through the door panting and frantically telling him what had just happened along with what had already been happening. The director said he would look into it and handle it. "Just make an appointment with my secretary and we'll get down to the bottom of it," he said. He never handled it, and nothing ever changed. They left me no other option. **God helped me to be fierce and file a sexual harassment complaint against my supervisor.**

The first lawyer I hired decided that for

whatever reason, she was not the person for the case. She had not done much at all. In fact, Housing probably didn't take her nor me seriously. Finally, she just removed herself. So, I hired an attorney from St. Louis. He was a bulldog and a go-getter! His investigation revealed that my supervisor had been also sexually harassing, threatening, and blackmailing other poor, vulnerable female tenants who lived in housing. He would even use his master key to just walk in on them unannounced.

It was becoming increasingly annoying and more difficult to concentrate and do my job without looking over my shoulders. Quitting was my only option. But before I could get the courage to do that, something really crazy happened!

One day I was sitting at my desk in my office working on the next newsletter. My supervisor and the director of housing both came to my office. In retaliation for filing the sexual harassment lawsuit, those bullies in the boardroom walked right into my office, looked me dead in my face, and told me, "Clean out your desk and vacate the premises." Not only did they take my title, my computer, and my shiny mahogany desk. But my supervisor even had the nerve to tell me to leave my name plate on the desk. Now what in the world did they need with a name plate that said, REBA JOHNSON?

They worked quickly to remove me from the premises, too! But luckily, I kept copies of all emails, hand-written notes, documentation of phone calls, and a "job journal" at home.

I don't know what they were expecting little old me to do. But with the aid of some security person, I was escorted off Housing property. It was an incredibly sad day for me. But I walked right out of my office, across the walkway, and straight to my car completely with my head held high! I knew I had done a good job with the newsletter, supporting the elderly residence, and helping the young women work toward their goals. But my assignment there was just over. So, I walked away having just as much pride and expectation for something new as I had the first day that I had walked into my new office there! Eventually they also sent me a certified eviction letter kicking me and my three small children out on the street.

The sexual harassment case kept moving along. Finally, it was time to take depositions. My supervisor was first. He slipped up and told on himself. When asked about the comforter incident, he first said that he did not know what I was talking about and that no conversation like that *ever* took place.

Later on, my attorney came back and reworded the question, something to the effect of, "Why do you think Ms. Johnson was asking you to buy her a pillow?" My supervisor slipped up and said, "No… she was actually trying to convince me to buy her a comforter." Then my attorney asked, "Didn't you say no conversation like that ever took place? And why didn't she ride back to work with you?" You should have seen the look on my supervisor's face *and* the faces of other people at the conference table! He just stared at my attorney like a deer in headlights.

When everything was said and done, I had maximized my seat at the conference table and won my sexual harassment case. They had to return my rent deposit they were trying to keep, and my supervisor was eventually fired. Finally, the bullies in the boardroom there and Twin Towers were all in my rear-view mirror!

3

MADE GUTSY MOVES!

I applied for and received the Claudia Company scholarship. Then I made a gutsy decision. I moved to Arkansas with three children. I didn't know anyone there. But I completed my bachelor's degree and started working on my Masters. I applied for a job back in my hometown. Just as promised, Mr. Dan hired me as an elementary teacher, all because I took the initiative to level the playing field and get my degree. I taught at Lake Road Elementary for two years before being transferred to an Alternative Center as Head Teacher! I truly enjoyed both of those assignments.

While at the Alternative Center, I had an opportunity to take my high school students on a fieldtrip! Those students were incredibly smart! Among other things, we went to see the Loraine Motel where Martin Luther King Jr. was assassinated. Midway our trip, we went to the Mall of Memphis for lunch! The whole day was very educational and fun!

After teaching all day, I would go home to care for my three children. So, it came to pass, one spring night, my son and I sat watching one of his favorite college basketball teams play. I had to open my big mouth. I'm not exactly sure. But it may have been a game in the Final Four! Those guys were posting and guarding and running and gunning! Everything they threw up, went in!

So, I asked my son, "How would you like to go to college there and play for them?" I was just playing. But he said, "Oh yes ma'am!" I laughed it off though, and we just kept watching the game. Sure enough...The team that he was rooting for, won!

I didn't think any more of our conversation. Then about two weeks later, here comes my son, "Momma, have you checked on a job or going to school there or something?" By then, I had totally forgotten all about the game and what I had briefly mentioned. As far as I was concerned, I was just enjoying spending time with my son. "Ok, yes, sure... I'll check on it." Of course, I just told him that to shut him up.

But he was totally serious, and he didn't give up. He came to me a couple other times to remind me to reach out. So, finally, I took a risk and called the University. The secretary took my information and said that she would pass it along. "Well, that's the end of that," I thought. "Nothing is going to come out of this crazy call because people don't really call you back for real. But…at least I would be able to tell Sterling that I tried."

Surprise, surprise, surprise! I received a call from one of the professors! She seemed excited to hear that I was interested! I was invited to go and tour the department and the campus. Some people have to say things until they see it. I am one of those people. If I don't keep talking about a thing until it comes to fruition, somehow, I change my mind, chicken out, or a thing just fizzles itself out.

Finally, I made another gutsy move! I went and checked it out! After all. What did I have to lose? My daughter Annice went with me. As we drove upon the campus, my eyes lit up! It was a beautiful place. But I thought, "What am I getting myself into?" The three graduate students who took us to view the campus were very patient and answered my questions. They also treated us to lunch. Afterwards, I met with a team of professors who were incredibly open and accepting!

The University paid for our stay at The Campbell House which was a really nice hotel! They also paid for our meals. That night, I could hardly sleep. The next morning, we went back to campus so that I could have a final meeting with the chair of the department. It was very productive. She felt that I would be a good match for the program. But said that she would need to meet with other faculty members and get back with me on their decision. I thought to myself, "That sounds more like a secret club than college."

Less than a week after we got back home to Missouri, I received a letter in the mail from The University! As I opened it, a check for reimbursement for my travel expenses fell out of it first. Then I began reading the letter. It said something like, "Congratulations! You have been accepted into the Doctor of Education program and awarded a full fellowship in the blah blah blah blah blah." "Oh, my goodness, I shouted! I can't wait to share the news with my son and daughters!"

There were several things to consider. But I finally accepted the offer, took a risk, and made another gutsy move! My children, three other relative children, and I loaded up the van and we hit the road! Brand new place, here we come! We stopped along the way to stretch and eat. We sang and played road games. The trip there was so much fun!

After we got settled in our new place. I went to the University, got registered, picked up my schedule for classes, and headed to the Book Store. As I shopped around, I saw all types of items with the school logo on it and thought, "Oh wow! This is so great!" I knew I needed some highlighting pens. So, I picked up a couple that had a fruity smell. I unsnapped a couple of the tops and took a big whiff! At that moment I felt thrilled to be my age returning to a classroom!

After gathering all that I would need for my classes, I went to the counter to pay for them. Well, I didn't have to pay for them. I was actually going to put them on a student account and get them as part of my new fellowship package!

4

SET THE BAR HIGH

I was feeling great! I loved the life of learning. I guess you could say that I was a professional student. I had all my fabulous things sitting there on the counter along with my identification ready to hand the clerk. She types something in. Maybe my student number. She turned to me and said, “Ma’am, I’m sorry. But you will need to go to the registrar’s office and speak to them about your account.” “Surely, it’s just a small glitch in the system, I optimistically thought.” So, I kindly asked the cashier to hold my goodies until I returned. I told her, “I’ll be right back.”

What I didn't know was that was the start of the University "kicking the can down the road." When I walked into the registrar's office, I sat down and spoke to a guy. I used big words and excellent communication skills! He pulled up my account and this is what he told me. "Ma'am, you have a $3,800 balance. How do you want to take care of it?" I replied, "Oh no, no, no! I have a fellowship that covers tuition, books, and incidentals." The gentleman shared, "That may be true. But your department seem to have omitted the out-of-state cost difference. Just go to their office and I'm sure they will make the correction."

I had set the bar high in anticipation of getting all out of this next learning experience I can get! I went and spoke to the chair of the department. Surely, she could get all of this straightened out. On my walk to her office, all I could think of was going back to that bookstore and getting the items that the cashier was holding. After all, they had school logos on them! The department chair looked up my fellowship information and determined that they had indeed failed to add the out-of-state costs. *"Reba, I am so sorry we didn't add the extra costs and now our department is out of funds."* I just stood there in total shock! Finally, I was able to say, "What do you mean out of funds? I quit my job, left my home, left my momma, and left my church…and you are out of funds? How could this have happened? Well, can't you go *find* some funds! This is totally unacceptable!" The woman looked me square in the eye with no expression and said, "I am so sorry for the mistake. However, you are welcome to wait until you meet residency requirements and come back." And just like that… The full Fellowship that I was promised to work on my Doctorate in Education, was gone.

Like a zombie with my eyes fixed, I walked out of her office, past the secretary, then out into the hallway. I stopped and just stood there, numb! Finally, I thought to myself, "This must be a dream." I clutched my purse and began slowly looking around like Dorothy did with ToTo in the Wizard of Oz, wondering where in the world was

I? I didn't want to say the wrong thing or mess up my chance of an opportunity later. So, at that moment, I kept silent. UK never stopped kicking that can right on down the road, and I was never able to catch up with it!

I finally met residency requirements and went back to the university to take advantage of the Fellowship. The bullies in that boardroom informed me that the fellowship they offered me was no longer available. Why was I not surprised?

5

ALERT!

Nevertheless, I continued teaching at a middle school adjacent to where we lived. Another school year began. We had more trainings going on than I care to even think about. Each one just seemed to be a remix of the last not really yielding different results for the students. But I needed to at least, “be in the know”. So, as our department chair spoke, I heard her say something again that I should have ignored. She said, “I don’t care what you teach or even if you teach, as long as the student monitoring report that goes home to parents looks good on paper.” Well, here we go again.

Culture awareness is crucial! Afterall, I was still new, and you don't just come into a new place and automatically start trying to fix or change what you think is wrong. But you also can *NOT* fall asleep at the wheel and just be oblivious, either. So, I kept my eyes and ears wide open!

Sure enough…right off the bat, case managers were not following the student's individual service plans, and everyone seem to be oblivious or just really unconcerned. Sooner than later, again they began to also violate the educational rights of my relatives who had been placed in my care. I had no choice but to speak up for the children. But everything I said to the powers that be, went on deaf ears. So, I filed complaints with the state.

In order to get me to drop the complaint, the bullies from Central Office sent to me the first of three black women to do their dirty work. This lady came from out of nowhere showing up at my classroom door. But she seemed nice enough as she reassured me that the rights of my niece would be protected.

But I was awake! And just as I suspected, she had been sent as a henchman in disguise to get me to retract my complaint with the state. I followed through with the complaint and prevailed. It's not something that I brag about, that's for sure. I would have rather the kids had just gotten the reasonable education supports they needed without me having to fight so hard for it. But sometimes you have to meet the bullies at the round table to get things heading in the right direction. It was so very sad how many teachers and administrators all seemed just so comfortable with violating the education rights of children with special needs.

One day I received a call to attend a special preparation meeting with the school district's attorney. Another student's rights had allegedly been violated. The case manager had repeatedly sent home falsified cookie cutter monitoring reports. This particular parent presented proof that her child had had doctor's appointments and that the teachers could not have monitored her child's behavior when the child was not even at school. That made her question the accuracy of everything else that had been told to her.

In the prep meeting, attorney asked one teacher a question. All she brought to the conference table was a Diet Doctor Pepper. So, she *guessed* when she answered him. Then he turned and asked me the same question. I opened my gradebook & monitor folder and referenced them for my answer. Our answers were *NOT* the same. Bullies in the boardroom will stick together. So, the attorney said something to me that made no sense, "*Now Reba, no two different answers can live in the same room.*"

So, I asked, "What then, do you want me to say? If I change and falsify *my* records, then the attendance secretary will have to change her records too as well as the attendance people down-town and won't that look suspicious?" The bully attorney just looked at me in frustration. Finally, he lost that case for the district, too. But I will always believe that if the attorney had drilled the other teachers as hard as he did me, the parents would have worked with the school, saving time and embarrassment.

6

FOLLOWED

CHAIN OF COMMAND

A few years later, while continuing to teach during the day, I took another chance and returned to UK to work on my doctorate at night. I applied and received a different type of scholarship, which of course did not have all the bells and whistles that my original Fellowship was supposed to have. First, I took two classes, earned two A's, and made a few new acquaintances!

Then, I took two more classes. They were going very well! Many days, our grades came from group work and open discussions. All of us were very focused and engaged every single class session. There would be days where the instructors would be late to class. Sometimes we would get to class and find a note on the door that class was canceled. Some students even traveled for over an hour to get to class.

To my shocking surprise, I received an I (incomplete) and a D that semester which actually equated to an F in graduate classes. First, I went to the professors to have a discussion and to ask them to consider changing my grades. They each said, "no" and were firm on the grades that they had assigned to me. Then I went to the department chair who said individual grade assignments were not up to her. But they were not prepared for what I did next. I had no other choice. I maximized my seat and exercised my right to take the issue and evidence to the Ombudsman of the University of Kentucky.

An ombudsman is an official appointed to

investigate individual's complaints against maladministration, especially that of public authorities. From the day I received the acceptance letter to go to that college, I never thought I would be gracing the thresh hold of an ombudsman's office. But I did.

Good thing I followed through and contacted him. In fact, because I had followed the chain of command, his office did not drag their feet. The Ombudsman scheduled a hearing right away. I already had all of my evidence in a binder and my ducks in a row.

The day had come for me to tell my side of what happened. I was anxious inside, sweating like crazy! When the hearing began, the professors first made the claim that I had been given failing grades as a result of "missing assignments, the quality of my work, and that I had to leave class to take personal calls."

It was true. I was rearing my three children and three relative children who were in my care from another state. So, yes, there were a couple of times that I had to step out of class to take a call. But from time to time, everyone did that, including the professors. Sometimes they would even take calls standing up right in front of the class.

I continued to explain to the committee very calmly and thoroughly what had happened to me starting with how their Special Education department broke their promise with my initial Fellowship offer. It was a trick, a trap, and a nightmare in the first degree!

Then they shifted blame to the secretarial staff and the mailing system. The secretarial staff admitted that the office was being reorganized and that things were, "a bit out of sorts around there." One office person even said that the professors were having struggles with keeping things all together (which would explain their appearing frazzled and disorganized in class). At one point, the Graduate Assistants were even being blamed. It was a train wreck and a big, heated mess!

There was always a lapse in time for when

they returned graded work. I shared that too. Also, when I would send them emails about questions on certain assignments, they did not always reply in a timely manner or at all. In addition, I had available copies of all emails where the professors admitted that the department was "somewhat disorganized." I also had copies of my research pieces including my completed IRB form, and work that they had graded and given back, but said that I had not turned in. The problem was that they had failed to record my grades. The professors *never* took any responsibility for being irresponsible. The Ombudsman kept the hearing flowing allowing mainly the factual evidence to be presented. The hearing committee members did not deliberate too very many days. They all agreed that I had effectively followed chain of command and that the failing grades given to me were unfair and unacceptable.

They unanimously ruled in my favor to have the classes and grades removed and to place me back in good standing with the University. Unfortunately, they could not give me a whole semester of my life back, sitting in class, my gas expenses, and the time I had wasted driving back and forth. Because I followed through with making sure my records were changed, I was able to enroll in a different university with no problem. Plus, had it not been for the promise of the Fellowship, I'm pretty sure I would not have taken a chance and ventured out past my hometown at that particular time.

Thank God, that experience had not come to stay.

It came to pass!

7

I KEPT THE FAITH!

Meanwhile on my teaching job, the bullies turned up the heat! But I kept the faith. First, the principal removed me from having my own classroom. Then he singled me out, removed me as casc manager, and divided my caseload with the other special education teachers even though *they* were the ones falsifying data and creating the violations for the school. But I kept the faith. To further humiliate me, the principal had custodians to place my work desk inside the restroom of the seventh-grade pod.

When I was not servicing children in a regular education teacher's classroom, that restroom space was where I was told to be and work. *I had not signed up for this!*

But to not look *too* racist, the principal did not fire me. So, I started out the year in that space. But each time I went in there, the odor became even more repulsive than the last. But I kept the faith.

I became creative! Let's just say, the Librarian and I became better acquainted. Finally, I created an amazing work corner for myself and worked from there. Inadvertently, because I spent so much quality time in the library, I had the best year ever!

But I had two choices. On one hand I could wait around until I was given a "Pink Slip." After all, it *was* my fourth teaching year in the district, and they could fire me without cause. Or… I could quit and leave my reputation somewhat intact. Quitting would look more attractive on an updated resume.

But I had radical faith! I took a huge risk and

a third option. I put in for a transfer. All they could say was yes or no. Not to my surprise, my transfer was granted! And just like that. Starting the first day of my fifth year I was given tenure! This meant that now, I had all the same rights and privileges as all the other permanent employees! This new school had even hired a first-time principal! Sounds pretty refreshing and promising, right?

Well…I found out that *she* too was directed by the bullies to keep me out of loops and not give me any leadership, extracurricular sponsor type positions. In fact, those bullies in the boardroom even told her to "watch me." They claimed that I had inappropriately stacked my timesheet when I co-sponsored an afterschool program. What they failed to share was that the other person I co-chaired with discontinued working with the program and I had to take on her duties. These work activities took up even more of my time. I guess they wanted me to do her part for free…NOT!

Unfortunately, while spending time being another hench woman helping her boss bullies to "watch, catch, or hang" *me*, she should have been watching her own assignment. She was one and done and replaced after her very first year as a principal!

Her being removed and replaced, paved the way for an interim principal to step in. He gave me a couple of gigs that added to my salary. Things were going ok. One of the assignments was that of Student Council sponsor. I made all students feel welcome and that their presence made a difference! Students who typically did not get involved with school activities, joined in, and participated!

But this school was in a faraway place, away from everyone and everything. I felt closed in like I was in prison. So, I took another leap of faith! I applied for and got a new assignment, facilitating meetings for students with special needs! I was super excited about another fresh start! I had high hopes and big dreams of making a difference for all the children and families I would connect with!

There was so much to learn! But I was up for the challenge. Most schools were up for grabs. So,

I asked the director if I could be assigned to Macey Elementary. After all I actually knew a few of the employees there and felt it would make my transition go a little smoother.

The special education director told me, "No. I'd rather place you elsewhere. Besides...You and the principal's personalities would clash." This was the director's second year on the job. She had not been around me very much at all. So, what did she know about my personality other than what she was told? Nevertheless, I didn't question her motive to her face. But trust me... I knew she had a motive. I just simply remained steadfast and continued to master my craft!

It felt great to finally be able to work directly with parents. Together, within perimeters, we all could help make sure their children with disabilities got the services they needed to not only survive in their classrooms but thrive! I was clear about what I was supposed to do and was unapologetic about moving forward in my career! I was placed at two separate schools. They were on opposite ends of the town. But I was able to make a doable schedule and make it all work out. At the first school, I went through each of the student's files with a fine-tooth comb. Several files were out of order.

Many black children had been herded into special education without proper interventions in the regular classroom. Several did not even have written parental consent. I had a hard time getting the principal to help me make appropriate adjustments.

But finally, as annual reviews took place and I began calling parents to invite them to the meetings, there was a breakthrough and processes began to change slowly. Parents thanked me for the invitations and for bringing to their attention their child had been placed in special education. Some signed the parental consent form. But some did not. When they didn't, somehow it became my fault.

Meanwhile, at my other school, some children who had *not* been tested for special services were getting special services in special rooms. But some kids who qualified for services were *not* receiving them and were sitting in regular classes without proper supports and failing. So, when I spoke up to about it, I was reprimanded for it, removed from both schools, and reassigned. Imagine that.

Awwww SNAP! Can you guess what school I was assigned to the very next year? You guessed it. Macy Elementary! The very school that I was told that me and the principal's personalities would clash. But why? Why would she intentionally send me there? There were *SEVERAL* other elementary, middle, and high schools in town she could have placed me at. That is until I realized the huge workload I had inherited!

From day one, I was buried in paperwork. All student files were in disarray! The last facilitator left a total mess! I had to work all day and all night, getting little sleep, to stay ahead of things. I had never seen such a calamity! If it were me, I would have been fired! But they only reassigned that facilitator to yet another school to destroy!

While just merely doing my job, I uncovered an insurmountable number of inadequacies. For instance, some staff who was being paid to be special ed support was being utilized for everything, *BUT* that. Students who were not identified as needing special supports were being placed in special education classrooms. Students who needed interventions in the regular classrooms were not getting them. But what surprised me the most was that without parental knowledge and consent, several students in the school were being put back a grade, weeks *AFTER* the school year had started! The way I found out was that some of the students who were being retained were those in special education. It was a mess!

8

DID THE JOB

I WAS ASSIGNED

Problems mounted! Before I knew it, there were people in and out of the school investigating what was going on. The principal was trying to talk me into going along with her scheme to violate the kids and even help manipulate test scores. Now that I look back. That might have been the plan all along. Since I had been asked to leave the other two schools, surely, I would go along to get along with *that* principal so that I wouldn't be asked to leave yet another school. Then the district would have justification to get rid of me right along with the principal. Violating the children and their written education plans would have put my teaching license in jeopardy. So, I kept doing the job I was assigned to do.

Craziest thing though. If I followed policy and procedures and did my job to make sure the students received what they were supposed to, I got reprimanded. Plus no one wants to stand next to someone who they have been led to believe is "stirring the pot." If I went along to get along, my teaching license would definitely be in jeopardy. Trying to do a jig and a dance was becoming increasingly more difficult than I had ever imagined! I lost so much sleep. I even started having migraines and feeling really sick to my stomach almost every morning before heading out for work. It was so very frustrating! But I kept my integrity. One time I got so sick, instead of driving to work, I drove myself straight to the Emergency Room. I had my son meet me there because I knew the routine. They would give me a Phenergan shot and I would be able to go home and sleep things off. That typically did the trick.

This time, the most bizarre thing happened. I ended up in a mental treatment facility! From the intake secretary at triage, to the attending physician assistant, I came in direct contact with thirteen different medical personnel! The actual medical doctor lived in a whole different city. His name was merely stamped on my paperwork. Each person who came to my room asked me questions. I gave each person the same information. But just like the gossip game where the first person and the last person's information was totally different…that's what happen in my case. Finally, someone came in and gave me a shot of Phenergan.

Once the meds kicked in, and I was under the influence, the ER made arrangements for me to be shipped by ambulance to a different place. What started out as being a quick trip to emergency room for a migraine ended up in a three-day *bid* at River Valley mental facility. There I was. Suddenly caged up like a bird! They took my shoelaces, the string out of my sweats, and my purse which had approximately $40 in it.

I slept off the shot I was given in ER. But I didn't leave my room for snack or activity time. I refused any medications and food they offered me at that facility. I did, however, participate in one group session, though. It was not beneficial for me. I was just still trying to figure out how I ended up in this deep dark place, by myself.

I told one nurse that I was wrongfully admitted, being held hostage, and that they better let me go! But she replied, "If you keep asking to leave, we're going to make you stay thirty more days!"

On the third day, I was standing in the doorway of my room holding the waist of my sweats balled up in my hand. I was at the right place at the right time! I saw a doctor and yelled out, "I need to speak with you! It's an emergency…I need to talk to you!" That doctor made eye contact with me and said, "Give me a minute. I just got here, and I need to get settled." I continued to stand in my doorway, waiting for her. Nurses and techs at the nurse's station started staring at me and rolling their eyes. I can't make this up.

Finally, the doctor called for me to come to her office. After I explained everything to her, she apologized for her colleagues. Of course, she couldn't say that I was falsely imprisoned. But she did admit that I should not have been there. She suggested that I follow up with outpatient counseling to help me work through job related issues. But that she was releasing me immediately "without reservations or restrictions." And just like that. The dark place had not managed me… I had managed that dark place.

After my insurance paid this facility, I was still sent an extremely huge bill! Finally, I went to their business department and explained to them about the thirteen people I encountered at the emergency room, how they twisted my words, and like the gossip game, each person's account of my condition, comments, and diagnosis just kept right on changing. I also shared with the people in the business office the treatment and the threat I received from their facility. Surprisingly, the $7,000 facility bill, disappeared. I continued to receive the ambulance bill for a while, though. Eventually, it disappeared too. I returned to work and was able to continue doing the job I was assigned to do and do it at a high level!

That following fall, I started taking college courses classes again. This time at a different university. Working conditions continued to be very hostile and stressful on my job. I continued to move forward dotting my Is and crossing my Ts. But things went from bad to worse!

Simultaneously, while fighting for my own job, I had been fighting an education battle for my niece. Her attorney and I had advocated for her for quite some time. The case was coming to a close. It looked as though everything would come out in her favor! But my niece suddenly left town to go back and live with her mother in another state. I had not seen nor heard from her in months.

Until, one day out of the blue I received a call from her asking me if I would come get her something to eat and let her wash her clothes. I picked her up. Not to my surprise, the school district had paid for her to return to town so that they could finalize the case with her. They gave her a deal she could *NOT* refuse! She agreed in writing to drop the case that I started on her behalf in exchange for a paid hotel stay ($180 per night), computer classes at the high school, a walk across the stage with her graduating class, and a diploma!

Shortly after I let the superintendent know that I was aware of their shenanigans, he immediately had his central office bullies get my niece out of that hotel. They fed her cake and punch, gave her a diploma, and shipped her back to where she came from! She didn't even get a chance to walk the stage with her peers during graduation like they promised her. Once she came to her senses and realized that she had not made the wisest decision, it was too late. It was no longer my assignment. Very seldom do we get to see what happens to people who do people wrong, especially if the administrators are the ones who mishandle someone. But the superintendent replaced the two administrators who were responsible for the hotel arrangement.

9

INSPIRED!

Not all supervisors set you up for failure or are heartless hard-to-work-for, bullies. There actually are some who represent their companies well, supervise with integrity, and help others to meet goals and even grow! They are called **SWIG**, **S**upervisors **W**ho **I**nspire **G**rowth! I knew that if I was going to maximize my seat, master my craft, and be effective at supporting and guiding others, I needed to be supervised by someone whom I could learn a positive leadership skillset from.

Take for instance, my internship supervisor. This lady was fabulous, classy, and professional all day, every day! She gave me so many nuggets and tools and made me feel that I really was an intricate part of the education equation. "You are going to be a great director, she said! And by the way…Thank you for everything you have done so far."

Unfortunately, at the end of my internship, I ran into a huge issue! Early one Monday morning I woke up struggling with a lot of pain in my eyes! But I went on and got dressed. I was determined to drive over an hour to get to my assignment so that I could finish my internship. I got in my car and started driving down the two-lane highway. When I would pass big trucks, I would slow waaaay down, trying not to hit them or run in the ditch. Finally, I couldn't take the pain any longer. It was just too unbearable! I stopped, pulled over onto the shoulder of the road, and called my supervisor. "

"I don't know exactly what is happening to me. I can barely see to drive. Can I please make up my time at the end?"

I had not missed any days up until that day. But to some, that would not have mattered. I couldn't believe what she told me.

"Reba, you have gone above and beyond during your time with me. So as far as I am concerned, you have completed your internship. Now turn around, go home, and feel better."

When she said that, I became my very own inspiration! It's not every day that someone tells you directly that you did a good job. To actually hear her say those words not only made me feel proud of myself, but it also helped me to realize that the only person I needed to compete with was me and that I have the potential to do even greater things in life!

When I got back in town, I went straight to see an ophthalmologist. As it turned out, somehow, I had managed to get into some poison oak, ivy, or sumac and it had also gotten into my eyes. But I will never forget her kind words. Even now, they help to remind me that not all bosses are bullies. Some bosses really do have sharp decision-making skills, the ability to empower others for greatness, and yes even compassion for other human beings!

Meanwhile, on my regular job, problems continued to surface in one of the schools I was assigned to. Eventually, the principal was removed, and two interim principals were brought out of retirement to take her place. I knew there was a lot going on and if I was going to maximize my time and my seat at the conference table there, I was going to have to stay solution oriented. I was clear about my assignment and what I was supposed to do. I assumed others were too. Apparently, I was wrong.

Take one of the two retired interim principals. Not only was this man a bully. Towards me, he was positively, toxic! There were some teachers who did not want to do what was appropriate for the students with special needs. They only wanted to do what was easy, familiar, or convenient for them.

So, they would go running to this particular principal for protection thinking he would *make* me shut up and let them keep violating the kids. It was so very obvious that *that* particular retired principal did not know special education law or even what was going on half the time. He went right along with the agenda of others. In my opinion, they should never have pulled him out of retirement to help with such a mess! There were too many moving parts, and he didn't seem to be able to keep up with any of them.

At one point he even demanded that I stop including him on emails where crucial decisions had to be made. He just simply wanted everything to just stay quiet. But didn't we all? This craziness went on for a large portion of that school year. I did most of the cleanup without his help or support. I stayed focused and remained professional.

But then there was the other interim principal. He seemed to really know how to run a school and talk to people with respect! He certainly was a supervisor who inspired growth & superiority! In meetings, he always thanked us for our contribution. One day I looked up and saw him coming toward my office. I was so conditioned to think the worse. It was all so exhausting! This time was no exception. "Oh boy. Here we go again," I said to myself.

But to my surprise, he had nothing but positive things to say. He praised me for positively working with parents and being flexible to "shift at the drop of a hat"! He also thanked me for *always* coming up with great solutions, staying professional, and keeping our school legal!

This principal must have been alert in class when his college professor went over the chapter on employee morale! He was a bright spot in all of our day. Because he patiently worked with me and I worked with him, we were able to get so much accomplished in a very short time. He truly was a SWIG, a supervisor who inspired growth!

10

I KEPT A JOB JOURNAL

Most people get excited with new assignments or working with new people. I know I sure do! But sometimes we get so excited that we forget or assume there will be no problems or no alligators in the water. We approach new territory with high hopes and trust in the people we will be working with the closet. The two seasoned male principals were eventually replaced by a black first-year female principal. I was excited for her and looked forward to hitting my reset button! After all she dressed the part and *looked* like she was on fire with a twinkle in her eyes!

Her office *looked* inviting, and she talked like she wanted to make great things happen and turn the school into a wonderful place for students to learn!

Early in the school year, this new principal attended some of our special student meetings. We all collaborated well as a team, including the parents! She *looked* like she had each student's best interest at heart. So, I assumed that she was a person whom I could support her in her new role, and she could support me! She attended several special education meetings and even gave good input!

One day, I actually had a chance to formerly introduce myself to her. Even though she was shorter than me, she actually had the nerve to look down her nose in a snobbish manner. "Yes, I know who you are, she continued. *They* told me about you. But I told them that I would go ahead and *let* you stay here and give you a chance."

What did she say? "***Let*** me stay?" She acted as though she was doing me a favor. This was *her* first year in the building. So, I asked her, "Who were, "*they*" and what did "*they,*" say?" She quickly blew me off telling me that that was irrelevant.

I really didn't expect her to be anything but loyal to them. Afterall, *they* were signing her paycheck. Well, they were signing mine too. But she was the one who even brought it up about them telling her stuff about me. Anyway, it didn't take me long to realize that I had totally misjudged her just by looking at her!

From that moment on, I kept my guard up documenting every exchange we had with a date, timc, and whoever else was around. But believe me, I was so thankful she let me know early, who she was and what she was about. Nevertheless, I kept doing my job.

Each and every meeting she requested for a student, especially ones for severe discipline, I took care of in a timely manner. If I have to say so myself. I was a master at coming up with solutions and respected everyone's time. From time to time, there would be hiccups to work through. But for the most part, I was able to accomplish a lot for the students with special needs.

Early one beautiful Spring Day, I was having a good and peaceful morning! I was dressed nice as I always tried to do. My students and parents deserved my best. So, it came to pass that I received a call from Principal Jet. She asked me if I happened to have a copy of my job description. I was terribly busy. But I was instant! I knew that if I was going to maximize my seat and be successful on my job, I needed to be able to put my finger on important documents on a moment's notice! But that request was certainly rather odd considering the fact that we had been in school over seven months already.

I stopped what I was doing, made her a copy, and ran it to her. As I was walking back to my office, all I could think about were the things I still needed to get done before I left for the day. My copy of the job description was laying on my desk where I left it. Out of habit, I noted on my copy to be taken home. Then put the clean copy back in the folder labeled, *Facilitator-Macy Elementary.* I maintained a folder with that in it, and other crucial information to help me stay organized and for other facilitators who would come after me.

That same evening about 2pm, she called me *back* to her office. Something pretty heated must have been going on for her to call me to her office two times in one day. Now that I think about it, I don't think she had called me to her office two times all year. She just appeared to avoid me like the plague. Imagine the shocked look on my face when I heard this woman say…

"Hey, I evaluated you." I stood there, with my mouth open and eyebrows tightly clinched toward each other, totally confused with a question mark on my face. I finally uttered two words, "Excuse me?" Still puzzled, I just stood waiting on the rest of the story. The principal went on to say, "I have to finalize all of the evaluations in the building and get them downtown, and I just need you to look over yours right quick and sign it."

That was the craziest thing I had heard in a

long time. I mean this woman didn't have the decency to properly speak to me or even offer me a seat! But again, I kept my composure and reached for the form. Surely this evaluation was nothing more than technicality. Besides, the director of special ed and district administrators had *just* completed a job description for us. So, I just knew it would be satisfactory and pretty straight forward.

After all, what negative information could possibly be on it? I had done everything imaginable to make sure *she* shined bright like a diamond without a blemish in the department that I oversaw of *her* school. For the last year and a half, I had been working days, evenings, and even throughout many nights taking time away from my own kids to correct student files that were out-of-order and out of compliance.

I began to look it over. In every section of the evaluation, each item was strategically and clearly marked, "below, extremely below, or does not meet expectations." She had given me the most horrible review that I had ever had the whole time I had been in the teaching profession! As a matter of fact, the form she did her best to create did not even match my job duties. There were so many errors on it. My six-year-old grandson could have created a much better one. She had misspelled words, disjointed sentences, and questions that pertained only to teachers, like lesson plans, curriculum, and student assessment questions. So, I asked her, "Ms. Jett is this a joke or something?"

I continued, "If you were going to evaluate me this year, don't you think I should have known?" I was hot! But I didn't need to be accused of "attacking her." So, I was instant in catching my anger. There was what felt like a really long pause and silence in her office. In fact, I know I heard the sound of wind blowing through my ears. It felt very awkward.

Finally, she broke her silence, took a deep gulp, braced herself, and began telling me all the things I had done wrong. The majority of what she told me were complaints from teachers who had come accustomed to not doing do diligence for students with special needs. She had no direct knowledge of any real issues.

Then it dawned on me that she was the third black hench woman that the bullies in the boardroom had sent my way. She must have thought that she was the woman for the job in gleefully doing *them* a favor of handing them my head on a platter. Apparently, she did not know what she had signed up for.

Again, she requested that I sign my evaluation. Still trying to process this strange document that was starring me in the face, I refused to sign it and stood on my, *NO*! She began to studder, trying to justify what she was doing and that my signing was not that I agree or disagree. But just that the evaluation took place. She could not quite get her words or her lie together. But I stayed composed. I did, however, in graffiti form, write a comment on it, and asked her for a copy before I left her office.

I came to three conclusions. One, *SHE* had not read the Employee Manual. Two, *SHE* had gotten in over her head. And three… This attack was nothing but a set up and one of the manifestations of systematic racism at its best!

Not knowing what she might try and pull next, I instantly printed her emails off and stuck them in my briefcase to take home, too. What was happening had not come as a surprise to me, though. Oh, she thought she was ready. But she was *not* ready for me.

That evening I got my employee manual back out, dusted it off, and began refamiliarizing myself with the evaluation process and how to appeal one. So, it came to pass on the very next day I contacted Human Resources for the form to make my appeal.

Once principal Jet realized that I really was going to appeal my evaluation, she emailed me asking if she could have my copy of my evaluation back and we just start over. I didn't answer it. She sent me a second email saying, "I am new at this, and I just want to make sure I am doing things the right way. So, can we just start fresh? Does that sound, fair?" I didn't trust her. After I xeroxed me a copy, I took her the original and laid it on her desk. She didn't say thank you, kiss my butt, or nothing. She just looked at me as I walked out of her office.

While she and others thought I was only facilitating meetings for the students with special needs and being solution oriented, I was also keeping a job journal. Let me tell you. When all was said and done, this job journal and saved emails gave me the ammunition I needed to weather the vicious employment storms I encountered and to take my life back!

I got a call from the Hearing Officer telling me that "we" needed to get everything completed in three days. I don't know if he was trying to rush me, hush me, or both. He said, *"We are in a bit of a crunch for time due to district policy on completed evaluations."* Well, I don't know who, "we" he was referring to. But after I reviewed the regulations with him, he agreed to give me more days to prepare.

11

I KEPT MOVING UNAPOLOGETICALLY

I needed a little motivation for momentum! So, I put on some dancing music! Along with several other movement songs, I put on, "Aint no stoppin' us, now." Then, as if I was planning a surprise birthday party for myself, I began writing a list of things I needed to do, starting with the people I wanted to invite!

I turned my music down. First, I called the Special Education Director. I asked her if she would accompany me. After all, she had been so complimentary of how I got the school back in compliance. She said that someone from her office was already coming to the hearing but that they were coming on behalf of Principal Jet.

Next, I called the Director of Elementary Schools and asked her if she or someone from *her* office would come and testify on my behalf. She had commended me for the fine work I was doing with working well with parents. The director of elementary told me that she would be coming, but on behalf of the principal.

I really should have been discouraged by then. But nope! Instead...No means, next! So, I turned my music back up, bopped my head to the beat a little bit more, crossed those two off my list, and got ready to call the next person!

I took a chance and called the principal of the other school. I guess I was just a glutton for punishment. I had made sure his special education department was caught up and in top-notch shape, too! We had a very good working relationship. There was never a time that he called me for a favor or to hold a *"quick meeting"* for a student that I didn't come through!

Surely, he would be willing to put in a good word for me. But who was I kidding? When I contacted him, he told me that he would not be available to go to the meeting and that he had already contributed to the evaluation and hearing by submitting to the special education department the "issues he had with me." I asked him, "Issues? What issues?"

All of this further helped me to see that this whole thing really was a set up! So then, there was the teacher's union. For years, I had been paying into it. When I called on them, they were not encouraging or helpful at all. First, it took several days for someone to even get back with me. When they did, they sounded very dry and hesitant about accompanying me. So, I did not press the issue. Besides, I did not need that kind of apprehensive energy sitting close to me.

I thought about calling on a few coworkers whom I had helped to cover and disguise their unpreparedness in meetings. But I knew they were scared of backlash and serious repercussions from the bullies who sat high and looked low.

Not even *one* person in the whole district could I find to come and speak on my behalf. I mean after helping out in several schools across the district supporting children and families and facilitating in a pinch. Surely there would be at least one person. There wasn't.

12

I CREATED MY OWN DREAM TEAM!

Nevertheless…

The day had come for the hearing. I had my head unbowed as I continued to put one foot in front of the other moving courageously toward the front door of central office! I had created my very own *Dream Team* consisting of two people and myself! The first person who came with me was my daughter. When she and I walked into the building, we were greeted by the Hearing Officer who was waiting for us. He was kind and offered us water.

He took time to explain that according to the hearing rules, no one, including my daughter could be present nor hear *ANY* of the hearing proceedings until *AFTER* he or she has testified. We greatly appreciated him for sharing that. Then the hearing officer went on up to the room to wait on all of the other district employee attendees. My daughter and I waited around for the other person who had agreed to accompany me. In walked my Pastor! I briefed him of the rules and powerfully, we three went up to the hearing room together.

My daughter was the first person to testify. She shared what she had prepared to say. Then it was my turn. I was not the only one who had been inappropriately evaluated and treated unfairly that year. Most of the other staff, however, chose to just talk amongst themselves, tell people who couldn't do anything, and/or suffer in silence. Everyone seemed to have just quietly tiptoed around this big bully all year. But that was their story. For me, I had no choice. I had to speak up! My career was on the line.

While giving my testimony at the

conference table that day, I made sure that I focused on the district evaluation rules, regulations, and what I could prove. I presented the emails and documentation of where the principal called me the day ***of*** my evaluation, requesting a copy of my job description. I also testified that on my watch, there had been zero formal parent complaints filed and that we had met all timeline meetings.

I happened to look down the line at all the people who were there on the principal's behalf. Any other time, I may have really been intimidated by all those powerful administrators. But not that day! I felt confident, encouraged, and empowered!

Under oath, Principal Jet agreed to tell the truth the whole truth and nothing but the truth. (*But she did not tell the truth, though*). She gave her testimony of how I "had not done my job." This was the strangest thing, yet comical. This bully didn't even know what my job was… and I was supposed to be the one who had the whole school in an uproar. Left and right, she was handing out "Pink Slips," firing people!

In her justification, she expressed how some teachers were fearful to go into meetings with me and that I would not allow the school to operate in peace. The real reason they struggled to come to meetings was because they would not be prepared, period! What she didn't realize was that I had emails from teachers on the day of meetings telling me that they "did not have their monitoring ready." But I helped them to summarize so that we could proceed and meet timelines. She didn't know that I had covered for them because she had avoided me like a plague. I never mentioned it until the hearing because as far as I was concerned, we were all a team.

Nothing the principal presented at the conference table was valid or made sense. She may have had a whole line of cosigners by her side. But it did not negate the fact that she had no verification or justification for the negative evaluation or anything she said against me.

It's crazy how bullies in the boardroom will

write the rules, break the rules, or try to cover up the rules. I was given a chance to respond to her.

A) It was not the year for people with last name beginning with the letter J, to be evaluated.
B) I had not been told at the beginning of the school year that she would be evaluating me.
C) There had not been periodic conferences and review of my work of what she felt I needed to work on
D) And last but certainly not least, *IF* she *were* going to evaluate me, she would have had to do so according to my job description.

I also presented emails of gratitude from one of the interim principals before her, the Director of Elementary Schools, the Director of Special Education, coworkers, and my immediate supervisor, who was the elementary special education administrator. He praised me for student folders that were in order, how I had *"brought the school back into compliance,"* and just an overall job well done!

There they all were. The Director of Elementary, the Diagnostic administrator, who represented the special education department, and another co-principal., all dressed up and sitting proudly by Principal Jett's, side...baffled!

When I presented the email where she had requested a copy of my job description just hours before evaluating me and the email where she was asking for my copy of my evaluation, I saw jaws drop. They had such shocked looks on their faces. Either they had not actually read through any of the evidence, the principal had not briefed them too well, or she betted on me not having my facts straight.

Finally, it was time for the diagnostic administrator to testify against me. She was going to speak on behalf of the director, and all the others in the department who were in cahoots, and I guess the *whole* district. This woman had brought a *huge* 4-inch-thick binder of information and was ready to throw me in the fiery furnace or the lion's den!

But it came to pass that right as she was about to open her mouth, my Pastor made a surprise disruption!

"I have something I need to say!"

The Hearing Officer interjected, "Sir, it is not your turn to testify. We have to continue on with our next witness… Proceed, Ma'am."

The hearing officer sat up straight and tall with his nice officer outfit on and his bottle of water to quinch his thirst. But using the hearing officer's own rules and procedures, my Pastor interrupted once again.

"I'm not trying to testify. I'm not here for that. I have an issue with how you are getting ready to allow that lady to testify against Reba after the lady has sat here and heard everything everyone has said. You wouldn't let Reba's daughter hear any of the other testimonies until after she had testified. *THEN* she could sit in and watch the rest of the hearing. But now you are about to allow that woman and I guess even others who have heard everything, to testify against Reba. That looks out of order to me."

The Hearing officer was *not* ready for that! I think he was more stunned than the rest of us! It's crazy how bullies do what they do and operate in micro and macro aggression so much so that it seems normal. People are supposed to just fall in line and not question anything. But not that day. That particular day the hearing officer would have to answer to his own sloppiness.

Dropping his head, the hearing officer turned three shades of red and was speechless! He swallowed hard and looked back up again a couple of times before admitting that he was about to make a huge mistake! But one, none the less, that would have inadvertently allowed the diagnostic administrator and the rest of the principal's scholarly key witnesses who were eagerly salivating, waiting to attack, to testify against me!

Just like that! The diagnostic administrator was stopped dead in her tracks! She was told by the hearing officer that she could not use *any* of the information against me that was in her 4-inch-thick binder. Matter of fact, she could not testify against me at all. All that hard work she and others had put into preparing their case against me, was then and forever, null and void.

She was appalled and obviously very disappointed! She slammed that big binder closed, stood up in disgust, clacked her heels loudly across the floor, and slammed the door behind her as she exited the room! It's ok because at that point her services were no longer needed anyway. You should have seen her. It was quite comical!

What she and the others did not know was that the favor of the Lord was truly on my side that day! God had sent an angel to disrupt their agenda and close the mouths of the lions sitting around the conference table.

Deliberation of facts and findings were supposed to have taken up to ten days. But within three days, I received a formal letter from the Hearing Officer. Those who sat in the decision-making seats of that hearing all unanimously voted in my favor and I was able to keep my job!

13

I TRUSTED MY GUT!

I thought my struggle with my evaluation was over. According to the hearing results and directives, the negative evaluation in my personnel file was supposed to be immediately removed and my employee file was to reflect that I was in good standing. A few weeks after the hearing, as I was sitting in bed treating myself to Banana Pudding ice cream. A sharp pain hit me in the bottom of my belly! I got up to get something to sooth it. Then just like that, it came across my thoughts to make a written note to follow up with Human Resources to make sure that the negative evaluation had in fact been removed not just in word, but indeed.

You may not believe this. But right after I wrote that note, my stomach immediately stopped hurting! But if I had no need to get up, I'm pretty sure I would have forgotten to contact human resources and my stomach would have kept hurting.

Sure enough… the bad evaluation was there! Someone had dropped the ball. Was it intentional? I'm not sure. All I know is that it was in there. Unfortunately, getting it removed was a bigger ordeal than I ever imagined! But I was very persistent in making sure it got done! I went to the hearing officer to find out what the problem was and why it was taking so long to correct.

I cannot make this up. The hearing officer said it should have been removed the day of the decision. Then he scribbled something on a piece of scrap paper and handed it to me to take to Human Resources. They thought I wrote it and refused to use it. So, I went back to the hearing officer and asked him if he would just go with me in person to get it taken care of. He did.

There is power in trusting your gut! Two months later I felt compelled to double check. So, I went *again* and requested an updated copy of my employee file just to make sure it was documented accurately. They gave me a CD of my file. I cannot make this up. The negative evaluation was back in my file.

This was inexcusable! Someone was obviously intentionally doing this. But who? Who had that much venom and time to taint my file like that? I was determined to once and for all get it removed! It took me going to the superintendent to get it finally cleared up. But who am I kidding? I would not be surprised if that bad evaluation, along with the "side file" they passed from supervisor to supervisor, is back in there.

They finally drummed up enough justification to eventually remove me from being a facilitator after all. But for some reason, I just could not let it go. I knew I was doing a good job in that position. I deserved to have it! I spoke to the superintendent. He could not come right out and say they were retaliating against me for advocating for my relatives. So, he had them just give me a part-time facilitator's position on paper and in word. But not indeed. It was just to shut me up, momentarily. I was the only African American high school facilitator and the only person not allowed to go to *any* of the weekly or monthly team planning and training meetings. They made up some off-the-wall reason why I didn't *need* to attend them.

When I spoke to the superintendent, he supported their justification. One thing about bullies in the boardroom...they will stick together! I filed that experience away. But it dawned on me... Once I cleaned up Macey Elementary, my services were no longer needed. I was no longer an answer to an immediate problem for them. They took the workload they required me to do singlehandedly and divided it up between five other white women who were *each* given full salaries. You heard me correctly. They replaced me with five different other people and transferred me over into an alternative program to teach there. This classroom was full of unstable kids who had gotten kicked out of their middle schools mostly for violent behaviors. To my disappointment, but not to my surprise, the principal was the same person who was the high school facilitator administrator. It was such a racket. Others seemed to fear her aggressive bully-type disposition. But I was unbothered unless she directly bothered, me.

14

I RESTED!

The majority of the students in this new program did not want me to teach and they for sure didn't want to learn either. It was such a waste of all of our time. Most of them were very bright and talented students, too! One of the students had severe violent behaviors and should have been actually placed in a much more restrictive setting. He had already been kicked out of at least *two* other middle schools for physically harming other students and teachers. He was sneaky and had to be watched very closely. I made a point never to have my back to him.

One day as I was helping another student in the dismissal area, that other student left his assigned area, eased up on one side of me and threatened to put a bullet in my head. Then he slowly backed back up into his assigned spot. I reported it to my principal and Safe Schools.

The so-called principal had so much venom for me. The only reason I could think of was so that I could not get close enough to the dirt she and others were doing. She had the nerve to ask me, "What did you do to provoke him?" She suspended him for only one-half day. Then he was allowed to return back to my class the very next day, like nothing had happened. So, I took that day off. Matter of fact, I took several days off! Taking personal time off when you need to, will help you to rest, regroup, and reevaluate everything.

Wouldn't you know it. Shortly after that, the makeshift principal, was also threatened to be shot by a different student. But she didn't just give that student a one-half day suspension. She expelled *that* student from the program entirely! Somewhere, along the way, a loaded gun was actually found in the dumpster in a backpack, beside our building. I never found out if the bullets in it was for her or me.

I started reaching out to other districts to apply for work. By then, I had earned my Director of Special Education, specialist degree, well over halfway finished with my doctorate, and was ready for more! Even though the goal line kept moving, the whole interviewing process was very exciting and fun! I hadn't had to do it in years. I interviewed with three potential superintendents.

One superintendent said he was very impressed and even offered me the position right on the spot! We decided that I would come to his district for a visit so that I could make sure it would be a good fit for me. When I didn't hear back, I reached out to him. I did not get my name out completely before the potential superintendent aggressively interrupted me, "There has been a change of plans. I didn't just go by the references you wrote down! I talked to a few other people in your district and was told some stuff."

I started asking him questions. But again, he abruptly interrupted me, "Ma'am…I don't have to tell you that. I don't have to tell you anything. Just know that I went with another candidate." I held the phone back away from my ear. For a brief minute, I thought I was being pranked! Finally, I hung it up. That is just another example of how sneaky bullies in the boardroom and partners in crime, operate. Why in the world would the district work so hard to block little old me from moving on I'll never know. But trauma on my job seemed to be a perpetual saga. It made the bullies in my brain work overtime. Yet, my behavior reminded me of a battered woman needing, longing to escape her abuser but can't find the strength or a route to do it.

15

I SHIFTED

WITHOUT SHAME!

The district shifted me again. This time I was moved to a homebound teaching position. The supervisor and coworkers were supportive and so cool to work with! I thought, "Finally! The worst is over, and things are surely going to get back to normal for me for a change!" At first, I was backtracking all day long. But it didn't take me long to get my schedule together and get a workable routine down pat. One none the less that would put less miles on my body and my son's car that he was letting me borrow. Things were going very well!

Maximizing your seat at the conference table requires discipline and meditation. On my homebound assignment, I taught some of the brightest, sharpest, kindest students in the district! Ranging from K-12, I had more students on my caseload than I should have. But I had really gotten the hang of how to do my job and I just persevered. The assignment was actually pretty awesome!

There was this one middle school student whom I never had to ask him to turn in his homework. He always had it sitting on the end of the table waiting for me. He would always be prepared for class, too! One day I was gathering my teaching materials, preparing to leave his house. I stood up and his Doberman Pincher bolted out of its cage and attacked me! The cage was not locked, and his mouth was not muzzled as was required.

The grandmother tried to get the dog off of me. But that 4-legged creature was just too fast! The middle school student yelled, "No grandma! You're making it worse!" Finally, the grandmother was able to grab the dog by the neck and pull him away. She got bit in the process, too. We both were dripping in blood! Not only did I suffer physical trauma to my lower leg and had to take injections for years, but the invisible mental injury caused by the trauma during my tenure there was much worse!

I was neither able to sleep at night nor function very well during the day. The nightmares and day terrors totally took control of my life. I gained so much weight and my hair fell out on my pillow in clumps. I ended up so weak, feeling alone, and in a very dark place!

Shift happened and just like that, the season of my teaching career was over. I had spent so many dark days by myself, working and eating lunch alone. But it came to pass that leaving the teaching profession was one of the best things that could have ever happened to me! I thought I would be so embarrassed because I had not accomplished all that I had set out to do. But just like my son and grandson so often reminds me. I hadn't lost… I learned! And guess what else? I really do get to live my best life and enjoy my grandchildren!

The events and shifts proved to be steppingstones that catapulted me to my purpose, passion, and other great blessings! My strength, hair, and my joy started growing back! Weight began to fall off literally and figuratively. So many wonderful and even extraordinary things happened for me after that. I had an opportunity of a lifetime to go back to my hometown and help care for my mother. I've gotten to travel to many parts of the world including Punta Cana in Dominican Republic, Alaska, Paris, Holland, New York, St. Thomas, Africa, and other places. In the middle of the week, I even took a stroll down Bourbon Street in New Orleans! I've been able to go and help out with all of my grandbabies.

Along the way, and by and by, my student loan debt of $108,200.00 miraculously disappeared! I'm so very thankful that God has the final say of what goes on in our lives! He orders our footsteps even when we don't understand or know the purpose at the time.

I realize that from time to time I will still have bullies in the boardroom including those in my brain to box and contend with. I can live with that. But what would have been a real travesty is if I had succumbed to the treatment, not stood up for myself, not kept a job journal, and allowed the bullies in the workforce and beyond to get by with retaliation, discrimination, hidden agendas, and other coward and bully tactics that many so comfortably practice.

Nothing in life is more challenging, riskier, or scarier than to self-advocate.

But anything less is self-betrayal.

About the author

Hi! My name is Reba Johnson. I am a mother, a grandmother, a retired educator, a licensed minister, a sibling of 15, a Mary Kay beauty consultant, a difference maker, and a life enthusiast! I am also the author of other books such as, *A Time to Move, Go Team!* and *Roar Lioness, ROAR!* I have several degrees and other accomplishments of which I am very proud of! But not as proud as I am of my obedience to share some of my life's journey with you. Thank you for taking the time to read this book! I am thrilled and honored that you did!

Blessings,

Reba

Made in the USA
Monee, IL
13 June 2026

54028577R00066